THE THREE DAY NEGRO

𝒀ESTERDAY

TODAY

TOMORROW

R. E. SIMONS

ISBN: 978-1-63923-819-4

Printed: March 2023

Published and Distributed By:
Lushena Books
607 Country Club Drive, Unit E
Bensenville, IL 60106
www.lushenabks.com

ISBN: 978-1-63923-819-4

Introduction

Whence Cometh Thou?

In the anxious hearts of mankind,
   Of what ever race or creed,
There's a throb in many a heart beat,
   And a great desire to read.

There are longings implanted,
   Inexpressible to state,
To pierce the darken vail of time,
   That so broadly separates.

To know of his descendents,
   And how he came to be,
Though all of one great family,
   Of different ancesty.

Ere we fain would know the future,
   It is good to know the past,
So a journey now through history,
   Will the problem solve at last.

As we finger now its pages,
   Which conveys the story true.
Of all nations, kindred, people,
   May it now reveal to you.

'Tis a question of importance, -
   On the anxious hearts of man

Tell me quickly give the answer,
  Whence came the dusky sons of Ham?.

'Tis the question they're asking,
  And the Author's object is
To make known, to give the answer.
  In this little Book of his.

As you now peruse its pages,
  Dating back to ancient lands,
You will surely find the answer,
  Whence came the dusky sons of Ham.

Composed by Mrs. R. E. Simons

"He Came From God."

In considering the Negro of yesterday we must turn to the pages of both Biblical and Circular histories in order to acquire the most fundamental information concerning that great and noble civilization of remote ages.

In the dimly lighted times of man, we discover that the race known as the Negro, was making marked progress and contributing to the cause of humanity in a remarkable manner. He gave promise very early in the career of man, of becoming a leading factor in a great world wide programme.

Whether due credit to the Negro, and his achievements has been given or not, does not at all make void the inspired writings of God which give invaluable information as to His dealing with the Negro of yester centuries.

With these thoughts we now turn to our most accurate record the Bible, which sgives full account of earth's races.

Theeefore it is logical that we lay the most dependable foundation, upon which we shall erect our Negro structure.

Many have wondered and questioned as to the coming of the Ne ro civilization. This question has been very misleading to many people, especially those who have not availed themselves of the opportunity of searching into historical facts pertaining to the Negro of ancient times.

Let us refer to cur most accurate record of earth's races and center our attention on the dark race.

There are not any inspired writings, which inclued

the beginning of nations, whose dates are beyond the first five books of the Bible, commonly called the Pentateuch.

It has been widely promulgated, that the negro civilization developed from apes, and monkeys. These lower animals live among trees and swing by their tails from one branch to another. The Negro does not convey the idea that his ancestors were monkeys.

If we accept this untruth, it would be just as logical to formulate the idea that other races have developed from lower animals whose offspring compose the races of the earth.

Man is a believing being but it depends largely what he believes and accepts that makes him what he is. If he develops the idea that the ancestors of any race were lower animals, he has a false conception of humanity and his very existence is contradictory to such an erroneous belief.

Man was made by God on the sixth day of creation. "And the Lord caused a deep sleep to fall upon Adam, and he slept: and he took one of his ribs, and closed up the flesh instead thereof." Gen. 2 : 21. "And the rib which the Lord God had taken from man, made he a woman, and brought her unto the man." Gen. 2 : 22

The offspring of that first family has developed into the present races, and the Negro is a part of that offspring. "God said let us make man." Gen. 1 : 26. "So God created man in his own image." Gen. 1 : 27.

One Blood

The family of Noah was of the blood of Adam, and because Noah was a faithful man, God preserved his life with his family in the ark, while the waters covered the highest mountain peaks.

There has been but one creation of man, and that was when God said, "Let us make man." Gen. 1 : 26.

All of the races are the offspring of one blood. Therefore the human race is but one great common brotherhood with one loving heavenly Father God. We do not have any account of children born to Noah after the flood, therefore the races are the offspring of the sons of Noah.

It will be seen from our brief survey of man that his language in the beginning was spoken in one tongue, that is every man spoke the same language in all parts of the inhabited world. This language continued in one tongue for a period of some 1786 years. "And the whole earth was one language and one speech." Gen. 1 : 11.

It seems unfortunate that man does not as a whole possess the original language. Can it be that sin has so bound mankind that he has lost the original language. Why do some speak one language and some another How can one nation understand the language of another How came the complexity of tongues? The reader wil now note just how it all took place.

Babel's Broken Walls

To repeople the desolate earth, which the flood had so lately swept from it's moral corruption. God had preserved but one family, the house-hold of Noah.

In Shem, Hem and Japhet, who were sons of Noah, were to be the founders of the human race, was foreshadowed the character of their prosperity.

Leaving the mountain where the Ark had rested, there three great families journeye to the plains of Shinar, on .he bank of the river Euphrates they were attracted by the beauty of the situation and upon this plain they detertermined to make their home.

Here they decided to build a city, and in it a tower of such stupendous height as should render it the wonder of the world.

This city was to become the metropolis of a universal empire, its glory would command the admiration and homage of the world, and render the founders illustrious.

The magnificent tower reaching to the heavens was intended to stand as a monument of power, and wisdom of its builders perpetuating their fame to the latest generation of men.

Josephus account of the town of Babel is as follows. The three sons of Noah, Shem, Ham and Japhet horn one hundred years before the deluge.

God had said that they should separate in colonies.

It was Nimrod who excited the people to turn from the command of God. He was the grandson of Ham (a Negro) the son of Noah a bold man, and of great strength of hand.

The Bible calls hi n "Nimrod the mighty hunter,"

and the beginning of his kingdom was Babel, on the plains of Shinar.

GOD TOUCHED THEIR TONGUES

Suddenly the work that had been advancing so prosperously was checked. Angels were sent to bring to naught the purpose of the builders. The tower had reached a lofty height, and it was impossible for the workmen at the top to communicate directly with those at the base, therefore men were stationed at different points each to receive and report to the next below him.

As messages were thus passing from one to another, the language was confounded so that material was called for which was not needed. Confusion and dismay followed all work came to a stand-still.

Lightning from heaven as an evidence of God's displeasure, broke off the upper portion of the tower and cast it to the ground.

Up to this time there was but one language, but God touched their tongues causing them to speak various languages. However the Lord did not destroy them, but scattered them thence upon the face of the earth. "And they left off to build the city. Gen. ii: 8.

Then followed the groups according to the three sons of Noah: Shem, Ham, and Japhet. Among these sons the Hamitic families founded themselves as a distinct people. Nevertheless they were all one blood.

After the disaster men began to scatter making settlements according to their speech in the afore uninhabited portions of the earth.

The family of Shem journeyed Eastward, the family of Japhet, journeyed Northward, while the family of Ham journed Southward, toward the hot section of the earth. The land where Ham settled was called (Ethiopia). "The children of Ham (Negro) possessed the land of Syria and Amanus and the mountains of Libianus; seizing upon all that was upon the sea keeping it as their own."

—Josephus— For further Study.

Albert Leighton Rawson in his Pronouncing Bible Dictionary, makes the matter of location more definite by giving modern names of the various countries over which 'they spread'.

He says: "The sons and grandsons of Ham located in Egypt, Abyssinia, on the South-west coast of the Red Sea, in Arabia, Persia, Ethiopia, Shinar, Chaldea, West Africa, Marcotis, Libia, Memphis, Thebes, Pathros, Sidon and Tyre.

The location of what we know specifically of the Negro race was the valley of Senegal, Gambia and the Niger."

CITIES OF THE BLACK MAN

"And Cush begat Nimrod he began to be a mighty one in the earth." Gen. 10: 8.

"And the beginning of his kingdom was Babel, and Erech, Accad and Calneh in the land of Shinar."

Gen. 10. 70.

Out of that land went forth Asshur and built Nineveh and the city Rehoboth and Calah: the same is a great city.

Gen 10: 11, 12.

At the commencement of history, and nations the sons of Ham gave promise of becoming the most powerful and influential. Among them arose the first great monarchies of Babel Egypt; the ancient and powerful tribes that occupied the Eastern shore of the Mediterranean. The cities of Sidon and Tyre with the Philistines were of that race.

There remains today little, if any at all of the glory that shone from these ancient cities of the yesterday Negro. They have fallen and wasted away. We during this age are reading the history of the mightiest Negro period of all time.

"EARLY GOVERNMENT"

After the death of Abraham his descendents by Isaac and Jacob remained in the land of Canaan till the third generation, and moved to Egypt settling in the land of Goshen for some four hundred years, after this period, God would then bring them out of Egypt to the promise land. Gen. 15: 13-16.

Egypt had by this time become a great kingdom governed by kings who had the general title of Pharaoh. The power which this kingdom had attained may be estimated by the fact that there was a standing army prepared to defend itself against invasion by the enemy.

The record says that one king had six hundred chariots of war.

Some five hundred years after the settlement of the

Israelites in Palestine, they adopted a monarchial government. During the whole of this period, Egypt seems to have been the most illustrious kingdom on earth, at least so far as western historians are able to determine.

On the days of Solomon it was in alliance with the Israelitish monarchy. Solomon having married the daughter of the king of Egypt. Of its greatness during this period it has left imperishable monuments in the enormous files of buildings and collosal statues that still exist in upper and lower Egypt.

THE NEGRO IN ANCIENT BATTLES

"Soon after the Jewish Nation left Egypt, and as they drew nigh the Red Sea, they saw the Armies of Egypt pursuing them as they were encamped beside Riharioth before Baalzephon." Ex. 14. 9.

With hearts of terror the Isralites cried unto God, their cries reached Heaven, they marched down to the Red Sea, and Moses stretched forth his rod, and the waters rolled back, the Isralites marched safely to the other side.

The Egyptians followed the path of the Isralites but the same hand that caused the waters to roll back detained the Egyptian host in the midst of the sea. There was not a soldier left, all were drowned. This is one of the most tragic occurances that has ever taken place in history.

A second great company of Egyptian Armies is brought to our attention in the battle against King Rhoboam, who after establishing his kingdom forsook God.

In the fifth year of his reign B. C. 975. "He

came up against Jerusalem because they had transgressed against the Lord.　II Chro. 12. 2.

With twelve thousand chariots and three score thousand horsemen, and the people were without number that came with him out of Egypt: the Lubims, the Sunkkims and the Egyptians.　II Chro. 12. 3.

Another military power coming upon the scene was Zerah who.se men numbered a million. The military forces of Zerah were perhaps equal to that of Darius who was defeated by Alexander in the year B. C. 331 at Arbela.

"SCIENTIFIC ACHIEVEMENTS"

Among the many achievements of the ancient Egyptians is shown by their skill in preserving their dead, a science which is today lost to the world.

The Hamatic race studied the heavenly bodies which gave them a knowledge of Astronomy. "One of the greatest contributions to the field of science was their fixing the length of the year at ?65 days."

Penetrating some 300 years and more before the birth of Christ, the Egyptian calendar was devised, by it the year was divided into twelve months of thirty days each and five holidays at each year.

"History gives the following account." The art of writing originated in Egypt. The first rudiments of writing was nothing more than marks on the walls of mud houses."

They later devised an Alphabet of twenty four letters, and could write any word in their language.

To every Negro whose mind reflects back over the

past and almost forgotten ages, he is reminded that the Negro of yesterday developed in the Nile Valley; the first great civilization in the World's history.

Therefore all races are indebted to the Negro for these achievements.

"A HIGH MORAL STANDARD"

Notwithstanding the blindness of the people on the Nile, as far as worshiping God was concerned, there seems to have been a very high moral code of living among the people. In fact throughout the East our ancient Negroes have always held aloft certain legitimate rights in connection with their worship, which are upheld by the races of earth in all christian lands.

Here are a few of the qualities which were to characterise the true Egyptian worshiper.

"He must never defend, nor commit murder, never blaspheme his God, never be an idler nor oppress the widow." Selected

No doubts no fears no sorrows,
  Within my heart now burns.
No discouragement, no interest smothered
  As I ponder o'er ages past.
Thinking of dark faces like mine.
  Who have lighted this world on time,
In their foot-steps roll
  The ages so sublime.

NEGRO WISDOM

We live today in an age when other races think little of Negro history. Their knowledge of his life beyond his coming to America, and the West Indies is greatly limited. His wide achievements have received little credit, but notwithstanding this fact there is inscribed on histories pages the greatest thinker of the ages, and this thinker was Solomon (a Negro.)

There is running through the veins of coloured people the blood of kings and if they could throw their minds back to the days of Solomon, placing themselves in his environment they would understand more fully the reason why he was sufficiently enlightened to guide a nation.

Concerning the wisdom of Solomon whose works come to us enfolded in the sacred scrolls are full of meaning and truths that lay deep, which is brain food for every reader of those marvelous, and striking thoughts.

"And when the Queen of Sheba heard of the fame of Solomon concerning the name of the Lord, she came to prove him with hard questions.   I Kings 10. 3.

And Solomon told her all her questions; there was not anything hid from the King which he told her not. I Kings 10. 3.

And she said to the King. It was a true report that I heard in mine own land of thy acts, and of thy wisdom.   I Kings 10. 6.

There is no shadow of doubt concerning the Queen's intelectual status, she must have been a keen and learned woman.   However when she sat at the King's feet her wisdom faded, becoming less than a shadow, even as nightly hours vanish by the breaking of day.

So dim and insignificant was the wisdom of Sheba's Queen in comparison to the might and knowledge of Solomon a master of mind [a Negro] of thought.

SLAVERY A HUMAN CURSE

The existence of slavery among national powers comes down to us from days of antiquity. There seems to be two main reasons for its existence.

It comes in the first place as the result of sin, neglect, disobedience and departure from God. Secondly, it comes as direct judgements of God. Very early in Jewish history the fulfillment of these main reasons were developed.

"God told Abraham that his seed would be a stranger in a strange land that is not theirs, and should serve them four hundred years, and that nation whom they serve will I judge, and after that they shall come out with great substance."

The early Egyptians held slaves. Israel was under their iron rule for four hundred years, until God sent Moses down to Egypt to deliver His people, and lead them to a land prepared for them, and their coming generations.

So goes the history of nations, slavery and deliverance, and sometimes complete anihilation.

As we turn our calm minds to one of the many subjects of political controversy on the shores of America, and and the British West Indies. We will find that Negro slavery in these countries was carried on in the superlative degree.

Amost every child of school age is aware as to how the Negro was first brought to the West Indies, and later to America where he became climatized to living conditions. In the West Indies the Negroes were successfully exploited so as to make these colonies the wealthiest in the in the world.

Just how these folks were trapped on their home soil (Africa) and driven many miles from the interior to the seashore is very plainly stated in Mr. Woodson's work, "The Negro In Our History."

The journey accross the hot sunny sands of old Africa was more than trying to the poor captives, and hundreds fell before reaching their destination, their bodies were left to be devoured by wild beast of the wilderness while the survivers moved on.

These captives suffered under the cruelty of their captors. Being crowded together in ships under the most un-sanitary conditions, poor food, and lack of attention, followed by fever brought many thousands to death and the ocean's bed was their grave.

Such was the lot of those who underwent that period of darkness when it seemed as if God had forsaken them.

"THE NEGRO CRIED"

Like every other people that turn back to God after days of affliction was the Negro slave in the United States of America.

During the beginning of Nebuchadnezar's reign, Judah wes carried away into slavery, and remaining in Babylon for seventy years.

But Darius the Mede overpowered the Babylonians in 538 B. C. These captives were set free and sent back to Jerusalem, with special directions from the Persian authorities to rebuild Jerusalem.

The miraculous hand of God has also been seen as He delivered the Negro from slavery. Biblical and circular histories, are not divided concerning those whom God hears.

The Negro cried continually up from Dixie of old, away in some barn, or solitary cave the cries of those who believed in God, turned upward as the tree top turns toward the sun.

True to God, true to himself, true to his master was the faithful slave. Notwithstanding the inhumantarian treatment which he constantly faced. There seems to have been hidden away in his being an unshaken faith in God, that led him on until the crust of unpleasant circumstances were broken, and the thick darkness removed. God looked out from his throne, and came to rescue four million slaves of Dixie's soil.

The folk song, the plantation melodies, the early morning hummings, and midday shouts of the (Twentieth Century Negro) on the cotton fields are but outgrowths of those, who with heart expression and deep grief, whose knees had kissed mother earth when the weight of indescribable wretchedness befell their pathway during the centuries of yesterday.

"I have had personal contact with many exslaves. I have eaten at their tables, slept in their beds, walked across their hot dusty plantations in order that I might bring them something concerning the advancement of our race."

The shortage of space in this pamphlet prevents my dealing on this subject at length, but will be discussed in its fullness in my next volume which will contain the subjects listed in the back page of this work.

Part II

Today

RISING AND SHINING

Coming out of the Reconstruction was a nation within a nation with new opportunities, which lay in the path of the Negro.

As he began to rise he was privileged to care for, and support his family, to educate his children, to take part in governmental affairs, and enjoy the blesings of his community.

Negroes began to graduate from universities showing competent leadership among their own group, however, those who gave heed to men of keen sight went west where their advantages were greater.

Men like R. T. Green, J. N. Langston, J. C. Price and J. W. Simmons were swift footed in bringing about better conditions for their rising brother. Those who were alert followed the advice of their heroic leaders, but some were well satisfied to drudge out their existence on the plantation, living very much the same as they did before the emancipation.

Negroes who migrated West, and North, as results of their geographical positions, their social interminglings, their educational standards, and none segregation in many avenues have placed them on a foundation of common respect. Their ability is unquestionable and their services are generally appreciated.

When the doors of such institutions as Hampton;. Tuskegee, Fisk, Spellma and other growing institutions' that are now world famous, began their work. Little did. the founders dream of the work expanding to such lengths, heights, and depths as we see to-day in behalf. of coloured people.-

THE NEGRO IN BUSINESS

"When the National Negro Business League was, organized by Dr. Booker T. Washington, in 1899 in that year it was reported that capital invested in strictly Negro enterprises amounted to $9,000,000. It was high time for Negro business men to organize.

Since that first meeting in 1899 regular conventions have been held annually in various parts of the country,. and the League has served as a source of inspiration and information. Such men as Dr. Booker T. Washington, Hon. J. C. Naiper and R. R. Moton have served as its president.

When the Negro League was organized Negroes owned and operated 20,000 business enterprises. Now it is two billions. The Business League had a very large part in this astounding progress..

Scholarships have been established at many of the leading business colleges for young men and women of our group to prepare themselves more thoroughly for business career.-

The Negro National Finance Corporation was conceived by Dr. Moton, and his conception was put into practical form at the twenty-fifth annual meeting of the

Business League. The purpose of the Finance Corporation is to provide working capital for individual firms and corperations."

—(*Progress of a Race.*)

J. L. NICHOLS.

COLOURED WOMEN PUSH FORWARD

"Club work among women, until women made up her mind that her efforts to help in the development of the world's work were not taken into account there was nothing among us that could be rightly called organization. Questions relating to the home, the church, the school, and the State were all of vital interest to women. She wanted her home pure and secure. She held the church as a bulwark against indecent living.

So great was the zeal that almost immediately the National Temperance Association, the National Congress of Mothers, The National Congress of Women, the National Federation of Women's Clubs and other societies of more or less importance were thrown on the screen and the world began to take notice.

So began the American colored women to organize, so came into shape the National Association of Colored Women's Clubs which now has a membership of over 300,000 women located in every State in the country including Canada, Liberia, and Cuba."

—(*Progress of a Race.*)

J. L. NICHOLS.

The opening of the afore organizations are some of the factors that are at hand to-day. When the opportunity came the Negro did not fail to lay hold upon the day of small things.

What are the results? We find colored women ascending to the height of success in business, in profession, in occupations, and minor walks of life.

Statistics show plainly the marked progress since the wall of partition began to be broken down.

GOD'S NEGLECTED DARK SPOT

The darkest spot on the soil of America is in the Southern States. There remains much to be done in many avenues of life in this field.

Up through the centuries men have lived, dreamed, and died, statesmen have orated in the halls of Congress. Authors have written many wonderful books. Poets have sung about God's dark people who are very much neglected.

Unusual avenues must be trod in order to reach the lower class of colored folk in America. We do not say too much, when we say that many Negroes in the deep South have gotten little out of this century of progress.

Someone must show the colored folk that the price has been paid for their liberation and the Negro of to-day must reach higher, and still higher, but in order to accomplish this, we should strike the iron while it is red.

There was never any greater opportunity to lead colored folk away from their old slavish practices than to-day.

We need men who are willing to give their lives for

their race. We need young men and young women who are willing to go where darkness hangs so heavily.

One writer has said "The Southern field is suffering for workers. Will you pass by your people making no effort to help them, or will you with a humble heart work to save the perishing?"

Negro Children of the Backwoods

There are thousands of Negro children in America whose parents have been pushed back from the frontiers, forcing them to find shelter in the woods. Similar cases are found among the lower class of white folk scattered throughout various sections of the South.

Living so far in the backwoods and coming in contact with modern living so seldom, children naturally fall into an unavoidable atmosphere of local habits, and ·expressions, which has a telling influence throughout the life of these unfortunate individuals.

The daily papers are filled with crime, carried on in a major degree by the opposite race, but turning the curtain back and viewing the moral status of colored folk, one cannot but remark when statistics make known the low moral standard among the Negro especially is this true in America.

Part III

Tomorrow

AN AGE OF MARVELS

With the many inventions, achievements, movements, and comforts of this age. It is not difficult to visualize mighty and noble strides in the Negro life of tomorrow. Just as the Negro of yesterday, developed into the Negro of today, just so surely will the Negro of to-day, develop into the Negro of to-morrow.

There are facts that cannot be denied pertaining to the future progress of our race. There are some obstacles which must be removed before this growing race becomes sufficiently qualified to master the situation and problems that now confront them.

The chief obstacle which presents itself is the lack of education. This lacking has prevented our progress time and again. I hope that the readers of this phamplet will not fail to grasp the truthfulness of these statements. If you have children educate them. You may not be in position to send them to college, no not even to high school, but what I would suggest is this, labour to make them studious.

My many years in the Southern States both as student, and evangelist brought me in contact with various organization that have been launched for the purpose of our development as a race.

Educate, educate, educate our boys and girls in a most thorough manner they are to be the men and women of tomorrow.

If the Negro youth could realize more fully the powerful factors which are today in their path, and harness themselves to lead their race to higher ideals in the home, the community, and the church.

We would see tomorrow with its heroes. We would see it with powerful masters in earth's greatest age. We would behold crystalized on time's pages the works of the dusky sons of Ham embodied in the Negro of to-morrow.

The next issue of this work will come to you, in a beautiful binding titled, In Letters of Gold.

The Three Day Negro in its entirety will contain approximately four hundred pages including various illustrations of Negro activities and enterprises. These pictures will not be confined to America and the British West Indies alone but will include scenes of Egypt dating back to Negro history in its infancy.

The following subjects will be contained therein.

Whence comest Thou?
He came from God.
Creation.
Man.
The World Before the Flood.
One Blood.
Three Sons of Noah.
The Beginning of Languages.
The Rainbow in the Cloud.
The Walls of Babel.

God Touched their Tongues.
Cities of The Black Man.
Egypt.
Pyramids.
The Famous Sphynx.
Early Government.
The Negro in Ancient Battles.
Shishak at Jerusalem.
A Thousand Thousand.
Scientific Achievements.
Astronomy.
An Old Land Mark.
Who Gave The World Its Greatest Gift?
Earth's Races Indebted to the Negro.
A Very Religious People.
What the Negro Thought of the Year After.
The Negro and The Golden Calf.
A High Moral Standard.
Music.
Amusements.
Architecture.
Negro Wisdom.
A Great Black Ring.
Soloman's Special Guest.
Old Ethiopia.
Africa.
Slavery a Human Curse.
Negro Slavery.
The Plantation Negro.
Born in Slavery.
What The Negro Lost.
The Negro Cried.
Men Whom God Called.